Journey

Walleah Press
PO Box 368
North Hobart
Tasmania 7002 Australia
ralph.wessman@walleahpress.com.au

Acknowledgements

I'm particularly grateful to two inspirational teachers, friends, mentors: Liz Winfield and Kristen Lang, who shepherded many of these poems to their final form. A heartfelt thank you to members of my several poetry groups for their encouragement, to many friends for their support, and to my son Duncan, all of whom have come on the journey with me and are part of the story.

Publication credits

Some poems in the collection have appeared in the following publications:
Blue Giraffe Press, Prospect three, "Reflections on some numbers"; *Blue Giraffe Press, Prospect four,* "Solomon's seal", "To the lighthouse"; *Blue Giraffe Press, Prospect six,* "Nietzsche and the philosophical pigeon"; *Punchbowl: celebrating the Big Punchbowl,* a collaboration between the Tasmanian Land Conservancy & Bett Gallery, curated & edited by Carol Bett and Pete Hay, 2017, "Vombatus Ursinus Tasmaniensis", "The Language of Water".

Cover image: Mark Stansall

ISBN: 978-1-877010-58-3

Journey

Jan Colville

Contents

Jan Colville was born in Melbourne, and moved to Tasmania in 1946. She has lived in Canada, and France. Her inspirations are Robert Adamson, Mark Tredinnick, Mary Oliver, Billy Collins and most Tasmanian poets. Her poems cover autobiography, science, social commentary, philosophy and occasionally magic realism. She was poet in residence for Poetry Australia at *Jam Jar Café*, Hobart for six months in 2013. She has been featured reader at The Republic Readings in North Hobart on numerous occasions; and thanks The Fellowship of Australian Writers Tasmania Inc., The Republic Bar and Café and the Tasmanian Writers' Centre for these opportunities.

Start with silence

start where we all remember
let's call it silence

start with white
maybe a page
empty

start with a thought
call it a poem?
    no   too soon for that

think of a line
imagine no one has ever thought
or said that

hard

okay   know that someone has thought it
yesterday   a thousand years ago
tomorrow

and let it happen

choose a font
tap the keys
write it
own it

silence has become loud now
white has become black on the page

someone a thousand years from now
will recognise that thought that voice
and write the rest.

Journey

I set out one morning to find my self.
    myself

I wore stout shoes and a heavy coat.
I knew I would be gone a while.

I walked into the nearby village
looked in shop windows,
tried on a pretty dress
but I could not find my self.

I went home again
down the road from the village
the way I had come
towards the house by the poppy field,

pushed open the wooden door
and he was there himself
     him self.

I said I had not found my self
and would need to search further.

Putting on my heavy coat and my stout shoes
I set out on the road again,
seeking my self.

Solomon's seal

Eyeless, they've arrived in my garden,
         blind green heads, tight-furled,
         more alien than plant.
Hidden for months,
         forgotten.

Now they come through warm soil
to welcome rain,
sightless visitors, turning in all directions,
             crowded by lush hellebore and delicate cyclamen.

Eventually a leaf   and another,
then the sudden surprise
of a tintinnabulation of white-green bells
down slender stalk.

It's thought they link heaven and earth.

Some think King Solomon himself loved
these mysterious plants,
hidden at first,
             disguised, then revealing themselves.

Such beauty stops time –
         a small miracle in my garden each year.

How could I have forgotten that?

Fifty-three shades of blue

As recorded by Saussure's cyanometer in 1789.

The boy   a prodigy even then
high in the Alps   laden with instruments
      chases the mystic *blue*.

They'd told him about the void
a man could fall into
      high in the mountains

where blue becomes unfathomable black
        a secret
      he wants to know.

Climbing peaks he sees
clouds curling into sky
      sky slipping on mountains.

A tilt of snow by the lake
gleams in slanting light –
      another shade.

In the valley he measures shadows
ocean-coloured and gentians –
      the bluest blue there is.

Saussure   years on
spins his colour-wheel again
    counts the blues he's seen.

Today we give them names
    indigo   aqua
    peacock   lapis
    cerulean   cyan.

I see forget-me-nots splash blue
step into a bluebell wood
and drown in the blue of my lover's eyes

while Miles Davis
lifts the trumpet to his lips
and ten thousand
blue notes
    swing through the sky.

Horace-Bénédict de Saussure is credited with inventing the cyanometer in 1789. Saussure's cyanometer had 53 sections, ranging from white to varying shades of blue (dyed with Prussian blue) and then to black, arranged in a circle. He used his colour wheel to measure the colour of the sky at Geneva, Chamonix, and Mont Blanc. Alexander von Humboldt was also an eager user of the cyanometer on his voyages and explorations in South America.

Truth telling

The wife's tale

> *There is no one thing that's true. It's all true.*
>   Ernest Hemingway

I

Ernest Hemingway's brown eyes, set deep, take me in.
It's 1920 and jazz is everywhere.

In the apartment of his friend Kenley
we're dancing.
We've cranked the Victrola,
rolled up the carpet
and danced.

Months later we're married,
a garland of flowers in my hair,
a spray of baby's breath on my wrist.

We're in Paris.
He's Hem, or Nesto.
I'm Hedley, Hash and Cat.

Arm in arm
we're walking the streets,
dining and drinking at Deux Magots
and then dancing, dancing
all the way to Spain and back.

If we weren't dancing, we were drinking.
There was a great deal of drinking.
And that was the truth.

Then there was baby Jack — Bumby
and of course Pound, Stein, Dos Passos.

In the Alps we climbed the high peaks,
skied under steel-blue skies,
saw edelweiss, eternally white,
thrust through crusted ice.

In the valleys below
we hooked trout from swift streams
and picnicked on mossy banks.

II

It's Bastille Day.
Beneath our window
a clarinettist plays a love song.

I'm alone.
Ernest has found a new love —
Fifi.

Fresh and full of life,
she understands him.
Her lips are a new country.

I'm not supposed to know.

Outside, the grey rain falls.
The music stops.

I thought it would last forever.

And at the Deux Magots
Ernest is writing a new story.

Hadley Richardson was Ernest Hemingway's first wife.
Pauline Pfeiffer — Fifi was his second.

Around the corner in the wind

  I attach my cords, my sail
lock my feet onto the board

and let the wind and sea
tempt me   take me on.
behind the beach the trees
bow and twist   umbrella out

stand deep in shredded bark
and leaves   pressings of time

pressings of weather.
stones roll into overhangs   the wind

still whittles   while I
joined to sky and sea   this piece

of flying   too   am tugged to land.
the board

digs deep   sail billowing   and I lift
   hurtling   wings

                         wide
  wide   and still, returning.

always   stepping back
bark   in the clinging sand… it ends.

and above my head a hundred
  two hundred birds   small

dark bodies   trim their   own
black sails — forty, fifty landing

on a palm tree   barely
holding   around the corner

in the wind.

Into silence

the woman
my mother
        is silent.

a clot
a stroke
a cerebral accident
has rendered her speechless –
        silent –

and found me
roaring
shouting
raging
        silently.

for what's to be said?

she's here
and not here.

this clot has blocked the time
where words slipped easily
between us.

this small thing
in its heaviness.

I feel the weight of it
and long to know
her voice again.

but now
in the clang, the clatter,
the nurse asking again
if she should draw
the curtain

we are held
        in silence.

You want it darker

If you are the dealer, I'm out of the game.
If you are the healer, it means I'm broken and lame.

Leonard Cohen, eighty-two
        bent in his chair
listens intently to his latest song
makes a notation
greets his son
his daughter, his grandchildren
returns to work.

His guitar leans against the wall
too hard now for his fingers, his back.

Pain is constant   intense
but friends still matter.

Marianne is dying.
He stretches out a hand to her.
Knows he's not far behind.

    There's a lover in the story.
    But the story's still the same.

The album is finished.
In three-piece suit   fedora
he faces the critics.
Frail as he is   watch his eyes.
The years fall away.

    There's a lullaby for suffering
    and a paradox to blame.

One night   alone
his time has come.

> *Hineni, hineni*
> *I'm ready my lord.*

He's leaving the table.
He's out of the game.
Challenges us —
> *You want it darker?*

Leonard Cohen died 7 November 2016 in Los Angeles aged 82.
His last album *You want it darker* was released a few weeks earlier in October.

Maurie and Merle love clouds

Maurie, the meteorologist, loves clouds. He loves rain as well. And sunshine of course. A tropical cyclone on his screen offers a frisson of extreme pleasure. Not that he sees them often, located as he is far from the tropics. Clouds are his real love. In all their shapes and forms. He loves their names: cumulus, nimbus, cirrus. But it's their shapes – painting stories in the sky – that he loves. Perhaps a castle, a recumbent nude, a swan flying past. All these delight him. Have done since he was a child. Being outside is almost too much for him. He cannot take his eyes off the sky. A towering cumulo-nimbus or wisps of cirrus hypnotise him. He loves his job at the Bureau of Meteorology. Loves the three screens across his desk. The jagged rows of cold fronts. The images of winds racing past. Clouds forming. Ah. Clouds forming. Work is a delight for Maurie.

When it's time to go home, he closes down his screens. One. Two. Three. Picks up his old leather briefcase. Snaps shut the brass locks. With one last look at the other screens around the room, and with forecasts ringing in his ears he walks out the door. Walks home, briefcase firmly in his hand. Arriving home he heads for the sitting room. Places his briefcase carefully on the hearth, gently opens it up, then takes his favourite chair by the fireplace.

Merle, meanwhile, who also loves clouds, but loves Maurie more, is walking home. She's looking forward to a quiet evening with Maurie in the cosy chairs beside the fireplace. Their home is in sight now. Windows catch the setting sun. Her heart lifts. Maurie is home. She can tell. A perfect cumulus cloud has just emerged from the red brick chimney. She smiles.

Breaking news

You can break in, break out or break up.

After breaking the ice, and a break-through
you can break the news, break the story.

You can break even, break bread
then in a ground-breaking moment –
break down.

At break-neck speed you can break free.

Enough of this word play, Dear Reader.
He broke my heart.
I made a break for it.

Reading Shakespeare's sonnets in zero gravity

After Sonnet 59. If there be nothing new

Poetry here in space is different.
What's it even doing here
among the things we really need?

There's this sonnet.
I think we studied it at school.

> *If there be nothing new, but that which is,*
> *hath been before, how are our brains beguil'd?*

Reading it now,
the things we learned have gone.
The rules and rhythms,
the clear conclusions,
are ambiguous
as I look out at a sun
that rises and rises again
against the black wrap of sky.

Here in zero gravity words slide off the page,
assume new meaning.
> *I have gone here and there.*
This weightless line hovers, asks me to think a bit.
Where have I been and to what purpose?

The passion for his lover
that Shakespeare pressed into couplets and quatrains
floats off the page,
challenges my neat assumptions,
turns them upside down,
then weightless
allows them to fly free.

Our blue planet lies flat
beneath standing clouds
and we, sixteen times a day,
go round in steady orbit.

Like Hamlet my words fly up, my thoughts remain below.

> *for now I look on truth*
> *askance and strangely.*

No prim couplet can the truth forgo.
We cannot, will not, meet again, I know.

Girls on the jetty

The wind fingers its way into my parka this blustery day.
I'm walking in the park by the river
where I would play with Rose when we were young.

fractious blackbirds squabble in gums.
ducks inch into roughening water.
a flutter of white-eyes fly up, surprised.

One cheek, catching the force of the weather, is chilled
but somehow the sun, slight as it is, warms and cheers me.
Traffic noise falls away under wind song and sea-slap.

foraging like domestic chooks,
red legged oystercatchers
seem at home here on the edge of suburbia.

In a trendy makeover, a walkway sways out over the water.
Technicolour when you catch it aslant. Grey as I see it now.

memories flood in of two girls
on the old jetty,
blue tunics, white socks.

The river is grey-green today. Soft islands of reeds float offshore.

one scorching Christmas Day
we clambered through barbed wire
to reach the jetty and dangle our feet in cool water.

I turn to go back, offer my other cheek to the wind. The sun,
lower now, is bleaching my greying hair back to blonde.
Sixty years. Rose and I.

I have lost two husbands.
she has lost her son.
a white sailboat tugs at the water.

& when

& when

my son
was born

a little too
early

a little too
small

when he
needed

a gentle
hand

it was
his father

who held
and fed him

whispered
soft

mantras
into his ear

day
and night

& when

the time
came

to decide ...
the child

was his
more than

mine

After the poem *&when*, by Australian poet Rory Harris.

White

I'm expecting green
as we head to the lighthouse
along the path thick-edged with bush

but I see white —
a stream of white pebbles
quartz
that tumbles down the slope to the gravel path.

We three have come again
on a grey day
when the sky is low and heavy
leaning on a pewter sea.

Along this path
everything is white.

Branches reach out   weighed down
with star shaped flowers
four-petals-white
scarcely any green to see.

And covering a log
white petals
fresh fallen.

Then   round a bend
that measures length of whales
there's the lighthouse
rearing up white —
white
against a grey sky.

Emily Dickinson's Herbarium

Now in Harvard Library vault, AM1118.11

words slip off the page
paste   more than a century old
       barely there   cracked with age
        and still
       here is the light through the forest
       her young hands
       choosing stems, bare feet
               in the dirt.

at home in early morning
after dew is gone
       beside the flagstone path
       there's Lady's slipper
       sage   sorrel
       Enchanter's nightshade

she kneels for violets
       downy yellow
       sweet white
       early blue
   some a posy for a girlhood friend
       others gently pressed.

on tiptoe in the wood
she snips
   the tall Richweed
       labours its name into shape
       in schoolgirl hand
     Collinsonia canadensis
   Places it carefully centre page
       exuberant jasmine
       above and below
       and common privet
       made special here.

ink fades
words
   slip
      off the page

but flowers still hold
      rose   sweet briar
      star grass   blood-root
      delphinium   trillium

      lively Johnny-jump-up
      robin-run-away
      love-in-a-mist.

years inch by
seasons tumbling into
poems   poems
writing   rewriting
bundled up with string

the herbarium   left
in a drawer nearby
scented with violets.

      ink fades
      her words   slip
              off the page

at her death
the garden path
and the pen
      quiet
      and still.

      they dress her in white —
      violets and orchids at her neck
      purple heliotropes by her hand

then through a field of buttercups
and drifting blossoms
the grieving family carry her.

    out from the drawer
    the precious book
    is taken.

    under glass it's cradled now
        liverleaf   coltsfoot
        musk mallow frost-weed
        as fragile   nearly
as the girl herself.

    images   have been made

      pasted round the world

        I see but cannot touch.

    I want
      to turn the pages
    watch
    her hand on the soft
    green   cover as if
    she will lean to me —
                  in her child's
            hand   these flowers.

The poet, Emily Dickinson, (1830-1886) was born in Amherst, Massachusetts. She compiled her herbarium between the ages of 9 and 12. Discovered after her death, it was placed in the Haughton Library at Harvard University.

Wind

Everything's in the air this week.
The wind has slammed in from the north.

Ferocious
it's hurled itself against trees
howled around corners.
Shuddering and shocking
it's found every crack.

The wind has come
and like the past
unpicked my certainties.

Today
reading the paper
in the calm of a coffee shop
I see
the notice of the death of a stranger
who was my first love.

Words
in a paper
in a coffee shop.
Fragments of my life.

Will you favour us with a poem Les?

Yep.
Panic attack.
It's called Panic Attack.
And Les Murray folds himself into the chair,
pushes up the sleeves of his ratty op-shop jumper
and reads.
As he has done for years.
Sermons on rainbows and broad beans.
Song cycles on blue singlet workers
   cutting timber with brash chainsaws.
Or fishermen, cigarettes dangling,
   watching the wind-shape of their nylon.

There are quintets for friends,
an occasional urban poem –
Brisbane – *estuarine imaginary city.*

Last hellos for his mum and his dad.
Wedding wishes to a couple climbing
a new green hill together.

But mostly it's about country –
bats, lyrebirds, cattle
clouds, eucalypts.

He's got an eye for the ordinary –
the shower, the louvres, the tin wash dish.
He sits, relaxed, in his colourful sweater.
Wishes he could wear shorts forever.
(St Vincent de Paul, he tells us,
is his 'sometime tailor').
I don't know whether to call him absolutely ordinary
or extraordinary.

Les Murray spoke with Michael Cathcart on Books and Arts Daily on 9 October
2014. The quotes are, of course, from Les's poems.

Distant music

Choose an instrument, they said to my son,
they on the other side of another country
and my son aged nine and a half,
distanced from me by a sea of dysfunction.
In the storeroom, wide-eyed, he chose
the tuba. *Nice and big,* he later told me.

I imagined my child, thousands of miles away,
heaving the huge instrument onto his lap
and warming the cold brass with now firm hands,
teasing deep notes out of its sinuous coils.

The tuba responded to his touch,
wrapped its metal arms around him,
cradled him in sound,
became mother   father   brother who never was.

Years later, aged fourteen, wearing white cotton gloves
he'd spend long Sunday mornings
polishing its intricate buttons and valves.
His fingers would find each bend,
each crevice, of the great contorted length.

This boy, in the sprawl of his room,
would take up his gleaming instrument and play –
while across an ocean I strained to hear.

My mother's watch

has strong marcasite shoulders
a face yellowed with time
dainty hands
    stopped at five past four.

when I pick it up
and wind it
the tiny crown turns cleanly.

if I'm very still
I can feel
my mother's watch
in my hand
ticking
like a heartbeat.

Walking on the beach at dusk

Here the light deceives
makes sea   sky
sky   sea.

Clouds edge waves
then float
on mirrored sand.

On that shore
fine markings
sketch an unknown country.

Gentle hills
are mapped
with fine salt crystals.

Dark islands
washed up overnight
mark this new place

invite exploration.

But as sea swallows day
and night falls
I end my walk

and turn for home
where lights flare from windows
and all is clear.

Small town – East coast

I
Turning off the highway I see lean sheep
so still I think they're statues
until one moves a foot to scrape at the dry paddock.

They're newly shorn, but grey
with the relentless dust the drought has brought.

Some lambs frisk – jump and run,
still white – innocent of the dull mantle that cloaks their mothers.

A gaudy sign swings from a post,
invites me into this town
more usually bypassed than entered by tourists heading north.

There's an art gallery – third owner in as many years, I've heard;
a café seeking a fresh start.

Businesses are spread out along the wide main street.
The café's open, and the gallery, and the pub.
But some appear closed for good –
empty shopfronts, faded signs.
Not enough tourists, not enough work.
The young have left, the others can't.

II
The heart of this small town is the marina.
A good-sized fleet rocks at anchor.
Yachts pull at heavy ropes that hold them fast.
Dinghies are decked for now. Anchors rest astern.
Craypots are stacked, ready for sea.

A light breeze strums the metal shrouds,
generators hum, and radios provide a Sunday soundtrack.

Boats with numbers as well as names
swing with the tide –
T48, RF4, T52, 1492,
*Spirit of Maria, St Bernadette,
Stern Rider, Karma, Eight Bells.*

On one called *Dementia*
an agile looking man –
crisp white shirt, smartly trimmed grey hair –
tidies the already tidy deck.
Must be nearly lunch time, he tells me.
Not that I'd know,
I've got dementia, he adds,
gives me a wink,
and vanishes below.

III
I turn to go, and see behind me
on the grass verge a concrete boat:
stern, prow, and something like a bridge,
brass plaques –
A tribute to fishermen
'Forever at Sea'.

East Coast names –
Bolton, Parker, Higgs.
Roy – father of eight, died 1967.

Son, Snowy,
'43 years a cray and shark fisherman'
died 2014.
Like the others
'Claimed by the sea he loved'.

I imagine him – strong shoulders,
gnarled hands casting out and pulling in,
facing the storm,
and not coming home.

IV
Back in the main street, in a neat garden
behind a picket fence,
a woman in the kind of apron we buy at country shows
digs a hole to plant a tree.
Behind her
a lace curtain blows at the open window.

I turn onto the highway
past the arid paddock
scalped by hungry sheep
and head north again.

Battery Point

Filling the bare winter garden
of the century-old house
the persimmon tree
is heavy
with globes of summer sun.

What I first notice about the quiet street
this morning
is a village waking to the day
to buy fresh milk and bread
and walk the dog.

Across the way three dogs, tight-leashed
nose out the other callers to the post.
Their owner hurrying them, seems
tight-leashed herself, pulls them away.
Never mind, they've left their mark.

The sky hangs low today and scrapes
roofs, chimneys, eye-browed dormer windows
that keep a steady eye on life below.

Oblivious to the chilly morning
a family walks. The father lifts the boy high in the air
and brings him down
to plant a kiss.
The mother is one proud smile.

Small gardens enclosed by prim pickets
contain a straggling rose or two that need the bite
of secateurs to tell them

From the basket placed conveniently
outside the real estate office
a couple grab a property guide
and set out to find a home.

Around the corner a long trail of cloud
lifts and heaves,
settles heavy on the shoulder of the mountain
and waits for spring.

The wind that drives down the street today
sweeps tourists and locals alike before it.
We can hear two centuries of stories
if we stop to listen.

And then in the silence,
as the wind drops
are all the songs of this village
waiting to be heard.

Mrs Beulah Gundling dreams

Mrs Beulah Gundling, seventy-two, of Moose Jaw Saskatchewan
stepped back from her ironing board and sighed with satisfaction
patted her freshly coiffed hair
lifted the dress she'd pressed so carefully
and before slipping it over her head,
held it against her still *fine figure*
the colour of a prairie lark this dress;
                    grey dawn
light as a wisp of Spring snow this dress.
                    crystals flew
as she lifted it and let it fall into place
                    perfect
nearly ready now   final touch   her dancing shoes
                    conjuring Pavlova
                     red suede   soft to her hand   *so soft*
supple as when she'd danced for the world
                    when she was young
ready now   she stepped out   into the prairie night
                    where
light as Spring snow herself
                    young again
she raised her arms to the rippling curtains of light
                    dancing in the sky
fire and ice here on this cold northern rim
                    pirouette, jeté
joyously she danced   as one with the dancing lights
                    danced and danced and danced.

Vombatus Ursinus Tasmaniensis

I am strong dig. Claws made to dig. Hurl earth backwards out of burrow. This one baby safe. Warm in pouch. Warm burrow.   More burrow across field. Near my rub-tree.   Big moon washes field. Time to come out. I am night run to rich grass. I am slowfast. I am all run when those fellas come. Fast. Slow when grass tickles. Slow when I scratch and nuzzle. Sharp teeth pull grass. Good grass. Juice all mouth taste. All food. Feeding the little me. I am grass bliss.

Slow me when the rain has not come.   Slow search.   Scrape no stems, no roots.   Slow to burrow. Wait.   Don't call me badger.

Nietzsche and the philosophical pigeon

A pigeon sat on a branch reflecting on existence.
She was a wise and well-informed pigeon.
Having read Nietzsche, she knew god was dead —
not unhappy news to this learned pigeon
who loved liberty and freedom as did Nietzsche.
But she knew you had to walk before you could fly.
One cannot fly into flying Nietzsche had asserted.

Why am I here she had often asked
and not on a different tree
at a different time?
Perhaps life could be more pleasant,
easier.

Then again, being well-informed
she had also studied the stoics.
Very useful for pigeons, she thought.
It can be tough
perched on a branch all day.
A bit of stoicism comes in handy.

Which brought her to the utilitarian philosophers
who knew that everyone's happiness matters.

Well, she was happy in her tree
since the very modern fad of mindfulness
taught her to be in the moment —
every moment.
Made the branch seem easier somehow.

She could go on like this all day;
would bend the ear of any passing pigeon.
Or resident owl for that matter,
although he did not take too kindly to her lectures.
After all, he was the wise old owl.
Was this upstart usurping his place?

One day as she was reflecting deeply,
a dog in the distance
started to bark.
It barked and barked.

It was Saul Bellow's dog
so beloved of Salman Rushdie
and had very little comprehension
of the meaning of existence.
Obviously a dog of narrow understanding.

Stop barking, she told it sternly
and start thinking.
Open your universe to wonder.
All life belongs to you.
And if in doubt
a little dancing would not go astray she sang
as she flew freely and mindfully
into a clear blue sky.

A *pigeon sat on a branch reflecting on existence* is the title of a movie by Roy Andersson
which won the Golden Lion at the 2014 Venice Film Festival. *All life belongs to you*
is a quote from Henry James' essay, "The Art of Fiction".

Throckmorton the African grey parrot

pronounces his name with Shakespearean precision –
a skill worthy of a creature with such a portentous name.

He can imitate the ready sound of the coffee machine.
The *'your wash is dry and soft and wrinkle-free'* ding of the dryer.
He is pitch perfect with the bark of the family schnauzer.

Throckmorton lives with Bob and Karin in a suburban street.
He can call Bob in a Karin voice
and Karin in a Bob tone.

He loves to get Bob running for his mobile phone
say 'Hello, Uh-huh' then finish with the flat ring tone
of hanging up.

When Bob has a cold Throckmorton can chime in
with a snuffle a sneeze and a horrid cough.

Sometimes he's amusing.
Sometimes he's irritating.

But when he imitates the bark of their Jack Russell terrier
Jack
who died nine years ago
Bob and Karin stop what they are doing
and tears come to their eyes.

Largely a found poem from Ockham's Razor program *Bird Brains;* ABC Radio
National 25 September 2016.

A good friend

Lacking a husband,
my night-time companion
is my clock radio.

It whispers in my ear
when I can't sleep,
wakes me when morning comes,
tells me when to leave for work.

And often enough
I just reach over
and turn it off.

Mary in the black and white room

Largely a found poem.

Mary lives here in the black and white room.
All is black   or white
or black and white.
There is no grey   certainly no blue or green or red.

Mary was born in the mind of a philosopher.
Born and placed in the black and white room.
She was very bright, very bright and very bored.
So she passed a great deal of time learning things.

She wondered if there was a world out there
that was not black and white.
She had a computer
and a TV   black and white of course.

So she thought she would learn about colour.
She started with RED.

Very interesting she thought –
*Red is the colour at the end of the spectrum of visible light
next to orange and opposite violet.*

There are many reds.
*They can vary in shade from very light pink to very dark maroon or burgundy
and in hue from the bright orange-red scarlet or vermilion to the bluish-red crimson.*

Mmmm, thought Mary. Still bored.

Then: *red being the colour of physical movement,
the colour red awakens our physical life force.*

And: *red is the colour of sexuality*
it can stimulate deeper and more intimate passions in us.

This is getting very interesting, thought Mary.

Just then, a white wall that she had thought was just a wall
like the other white walls
that had locked her in
slid open.

Right in the doorway   a white marble stand
and sitting on top of this stand
an apple.

RED. *(colour at the end of the spectrum of visible light)*
RED. *(the colour of sexuality)*

Mmmmm, thought Mary, interested now.
Very interested.

Then Mary, in her billowing white dress
white ribbons cascading from her hair
white stockings in dainty black slippers
picked up the apple.

Cold   cold and firm in her hand.
So this is red, she thought.
and slowly, slowly
bit into the red apple.

Mary and the black and white room is a well-known thought experiment that seeks
to find out how we really know something. It is referred to in the 2015 movie
Ex Machina.

Going to town

Dressing carefully.
Precise grooming.
I'm going to town.

I think the clock on the stove is ten minutes slow
and the one on the bench might be a quarter of an hour fast.
I'm sure the one in the bedroom is wrong.
In the car it's still daylight saving time.

I don't really know what time it is.

Not that it matters.
I'm not sure who I am today.

To the lighthouse

In wild wind, I've climbed to the highest point
above the heaving bay.

On the path winding to the lighthouse
markers tell the size of whales.

Small-leafed bushes hug the cliff, surviving the wind
their tiny flowers   stars come to earth.
Tangled roots skein across pink granite.

I know this rock has pushed up
from the molten layers of the earth.

This is where I need to be right now
          high on this ancient rock
                          facing the wind.

In Smartland

Jeffrey Smart and Piero Della Francesca

I
In the water-coloured landscape of Tuscany
among hills weighed down by olives
beneath the azure sky
        Jeffrey Smart paints stark images
of car parks, factories, road signs
trains, trucks.

There's scarcely a person to be seen
in Smartland.
Sometimes the back of a road-worker.

One self-portrait –
Smart against a derelict factory wall
dark grey rollneck, baggy pants
hands in pockets
part of the wall
blending in.

There is, of course, the *Portrait of Clive James.*
Hours of sittings
preliminary sketches
then the famous canvas.

Huge urban overpass –
concrete, lunging over peeling orange walls.
A rearing blue-glassed skyscraper
and up there, high on the motorway
two hands grasping the edge
and a very small head –
Clive James.

II
One day, hot —
a heat that refuses to leave the earth
Jeffrey Smart aged eighty
frail but indefatigable
travels to Arezzo.

Here time contracts
the Renaissance is round every corner —
on every wall.

Smart can never see enough of Della Francesca —
his Piero. Centuries apart
they're brothers in art.

He limps to the Basilica
leaning heavily on his companion
eager to see the crucifixion
restored at last

borrows a ladder
climbs stiffly to the altar
to gaze with satisfaction
into Piero's face of Christ.

Ten long minutes he's there
precarious atop the ladder
in the cool light of the church
face to face with Christ —
and Piero.

Balancing up there
he's breathless   exhausted.
They help him down.
He leans again, stick in place.
His steps are halting — hesitant.

But look at his eyes.
He's seen something new.
In the face of Christ painted centuries ago
there's fresh challenge —
more to learn.

His pace quickens.

Painting: number 1A

Museum of Modern Art
New York 1948

The canvas, tacked to the hard wall of the floor,
was huge
and he, prodigious —
Jackson Pollock in the face
of the new world.

He would give this work
a name that was no name — *Painting.*
To crack the cages of the eyes.
To be here. Anywhere
the old world wasn't.

Throw away easel, palette, brush
wield stick, trowel, knife
with angry energy.

Flick, pour, dribble, spread.

The fevered pulse of his mind
makes skeins, puddles, threads of paint,
and finest filigree as well.

It's here now, years later
on a gallery wall,
a swirling, leaping, desperate dance
chaos defying chaos.

The language of water

at the Big Punchbowl

just debris, leaf litter, tangled banksia
dank mud that clings and sucks
ragged teatree, straggling wattle

not bushland
a between-land
edge of great water-bowl
      shallow
not beach   not lake
a country where
trees stand greenly in water
      clouds float upside down
on a hint of waves

a skein of tiny leaves sways
with wind and current
      a yellow flower brightly
reflects the sun   reaches for sky
      roots firm in muddy ground
      here to stay
in a water-world
I step into

      I've left the edge
tread softly in this quiet place
      I'm water now
my waterskin drinking waves
      drinking clouds

and deeper… the shore recedes

swans herd their young here
memory of hunters steers their course

a reed is gently wrapped
in swansdown

tadpoles swim the sky
tomorrow they will sing this place

my breath is softbreath
        a wake of bubbles blooms
freed from mud
shows where I have been
        will bring me back

an eagle   shadow against the sun
        circles   seeing me
        seeing too   a ripple   a chance
feet climbing cloud

by the shore — as I return — birds
have gathered in the wiry grass
birdsong threading stems

        At home
        my body wants
        this other world
        of water-rooted trees
        the drift and float
        tadpoles
        becoming frogs
        and the sky song   here
        in my mouth.

On the train

8.42 am
She's putting on her make-up.
Everything – foundation, blusher, lipstick.
Eye shadow, mascara.
She has a small mirror, and is very thorough.

A few tendrils loop down
from soft brown hair
piled on top of her head.

I can only see the back of her neck.
It's elegant.
I'm intrigued.
She looks beautiful.

Then, as she is finishing her lashes
I catch a glimpse of her face in her mirror.
She truly is beautiful.

If I can see her, can she see me, watching her?

The next stop is MacDonald Town.

Her stop.

8.50 am
They are an exotic couple
young – early twenties.
Olive skin, dark brown eyes.
South American?
He has black hair with coloured tips.
Brown hair touches her shoulder
and falls across her face.

He is talking, talking at her — insistent.
She is reading a catalogue.
(CDs and DVDs. 2 for $9.99.)

His hand is on her shoulder, her neck.
He fiddles with the pearl in her ear.
He pulls her to him.
She lets her head rest on his shoulder
then returns to her catalogue.

The next stop is Central

He is getting off.
She follows — slowly.

4.50pm
Mid-forties. He's standing by the doors.
Khaki pants and shirt.
Sleeves rolled to the elbow.
Black lace-up shoes. Short red socks.
Red backpack.
He has expensive-looking headphones.
There's a tightly rolled umbrella tucked under his arm.

Leaning against his right leg — a quite large framed print,
red background, with the injunction filling the frame:
KEEP CALM AND CARRY ON.
He looks calm enough.
The next stop is Newtown.
He alights — calmly.

4.57 pm
Older woman.
Tourist apparently.
Has all the accoutrements. Sensible shoes,
sensible bag to hold book, water, raincoat.
One of the few people on this train who is not texting.
She looks a bit tired. Big day?

The next stop is Stanmore.

I reach in my sensible bag for my umbrella.
My stop.

Mind the gap.

Reflections on some numbers

1

One is the answer to any sum
   says Patrick White in Voss.
   One mother.
   One father.
   One lover – at a time.
   One husband –
      at a time.
   One son.

42

Forty-two is a pronic number and an abundant number.
Its prime factorization makes it the second sphenic number.
42 has a 14 member aliquot sequence,
and it's the 10th member of the 3-aliquot tree.
Oh, and did I say 42 is the meaning of life?

I still like *one* as the answer to any sum.
Beats 42 4 me

Wattlebird bliss

There's probably a collective noun for them
these wattlebirds
energetic on a cold spring morning

>a chortle
>a chuckle
>a haggle
>a hurtle
>a huddle

plump acrobats
upside down
long tails in the air
beaks seeking sweet nectar
deep in creamy blossom

their silver grey gleams
in silver leaves
as they race backwards and forwards
choosing one favoured branch
and then another
from the eucalypts in our seaside garden

they nudge each other
cede to each other
return again
plenty for all
here on the edge of the bay

then — sated
they discover the roof
has become a bath for them
after last night's rain

      beaks dipping and pushing
      wet wings now glinting
      claws scratching to hold on
      settling to a joyous bath
      they make rain

we duck our heads
   drink — through our skins —
   this morning bliss.

Poet and painter see two birds

Two birds, black, pierce the sky, prey-call each other. A poet mouths their colour, hears their blue-black-blue gloss as consonant-vowel-consonant uncoiling; breathes a line as each feather wind-lifted determines course another call   another turn   a line. Here in open woodland, edged by shallow bay she steps in ancient footsteps that hunted here and wrote their stories with rocks and shells.   A painter sees the birds, names that colour, her fingers stretch and flex. Her brush right now would hang above the canvas eager   full   ready. But first she breathes the light these birds tore through   touches the wind that lifts the feathers stops that moment knows that light and wind and colour and scent of sea will become all bird and knows the shadow at the edge of vision is the poet who also holds that moment. They breathe together.

In the green season

This green stone in my hand has the chill of the north in it. But it's not quite a stone. It's a sculpture bought in the Arctic Circle, when he and I were still together. As I weigh it in my hand — as I often do — it's cold, heavy. We'd headed north, as far as you could go in Manitoba that last Canadian summer; still exploring, still hoping; and in a tiny store in an Inuit village there she was — tumbled in a drawer with other small stones.

An odd shaped block that fitted into the palm of my hand, she'd been relegated to the scrap box because she wasn't quite complete. But that's what I loved about her. I imagined the maker seeking her story in this ancient basalt rock. She - and she's definitely female — is an Inuit woman, hooded parka, angular features, two arms, no hands, and that's about it. The rest of her is still caught in the stone.

In these high latitudes, where winter is a blaze of black snow and the shimmer of the northern lights is trapped in green-stone, he takes her in his hands and patiently — for he has many dark months to work - smooths and shapes the rough rock he gathered on the seal-slicked shore.

Through the silent season he works on this green-dappled woman. I fantasise he wants to stay with her. Caught in the stone, she's his. Once out, in the green season, she's free of the weight of shadows; will be sold to tourists like us.

Then one night, when the wind blows fiercely and winter's nearly over, his woman, who has sat with him through the long time, reaches out her soft hand. *Come,* she says.

The small sculpture, not finished, falls to the floor and months later becomes mine as I turn south.

Language of love

Flora Sorella Garcia and her lover Gregoire Vandenburg
    fought fiercely and often in Spanish
    argued daily and vociferously in English
    bickered repeatedly in fluent Dutch.

But at night, in wordless dark
    their bodies met
        breast lay on breast
        heart against heart
        love met love

    and language fled ...